Strange Beginnings

First simultaneously published in 2001 in the U.K., Canada and the U.S.A. by Tradewind Books Limited
E-mail: tradewindbooks@eudoramail.com
www.tradewindbooks.com

Distributed in the U.S.A. by Interlink Books, Northampton, MA
E-mail: info@interlinkbooks.com
www.interlinkbooks.com

Distributed in Canada by General Distribution Services
E-mail: cservice@genpub.com

Distributed in the U.K. by Turnaround, London
E-mail: enquirie@turnaround-uk.com

Distributed in Australia by John Reed Books, Sydney
E-mail: johnreed@barcode.com.au

Text copyright © 2001 by Karen Needham and Launi Lucas
Illustrations copyright © 2001 by Launi Lucas

Designed by Carol Aitken

Printed and bound in Hong Kong by C & C Offset
Prepress by Supreme Graphics, Burnaby, British Columbia

Cataloguing in Publication Data for this book is available from the Library of Congress and the British Library
Library of Congress Control Number: 2001091970

National Library of Canada Cataloguing in Publication Data

Needham, Karen Merrie, 1963–
  Strange beginnings

  ISBN 1-896580-11-4

  1. Aquatic insects—Juvenile literature.
I. Lucas, Launi. II. Title.
QL472.N43 2001   j595.7176   C2001-910784-6

10 9 8 7 6 5 4 3 2 1

Tradewind Books gratefully acknowledges the support of the Canada Council for the Arts.

THE CANADA COUNCIL | LE CONSEIL DES ARTS
FOR THE ARTS | DU CANADA
SINCE 1957 | DEPUIS 1957

Strange Beginnings

Karen Needham and Launi Lucas
Illustrated by Launi Lucas

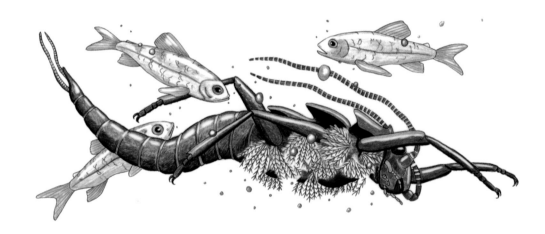

London / Vancouver / Boston

This book is dedicated to bug lovers young and
old who don't mind getting their feet wet.

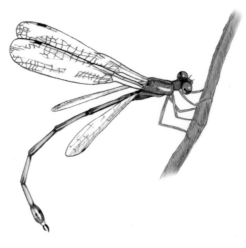

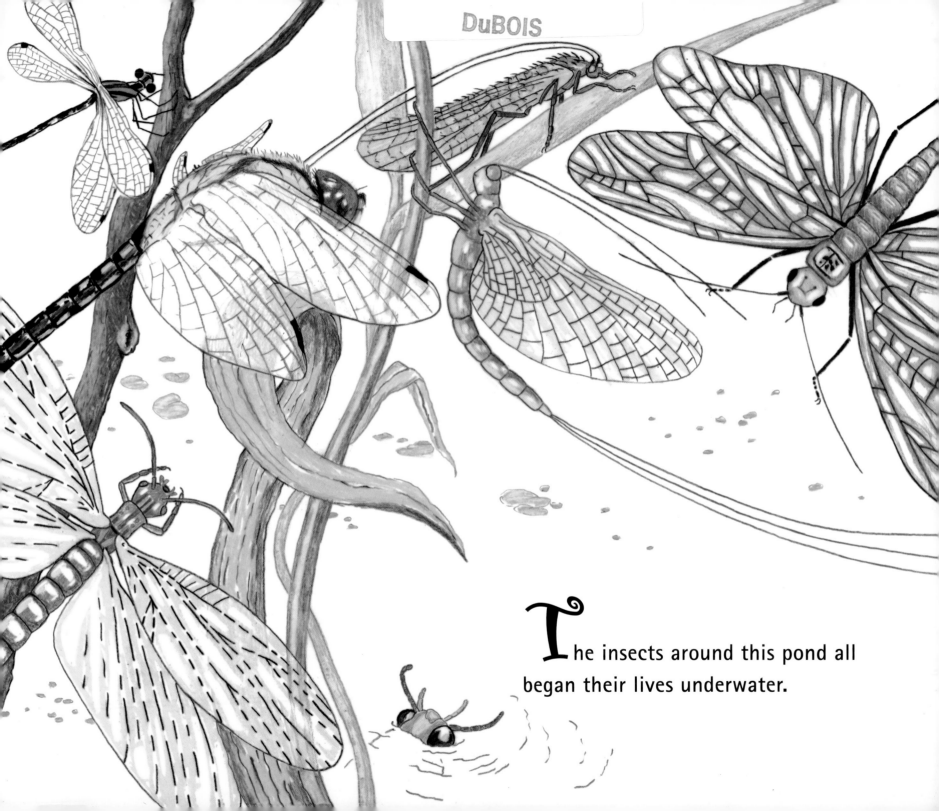

The insects around this pond all began their lives underwater.

*O*ften, young underwater insects look nothing like the adults they become.

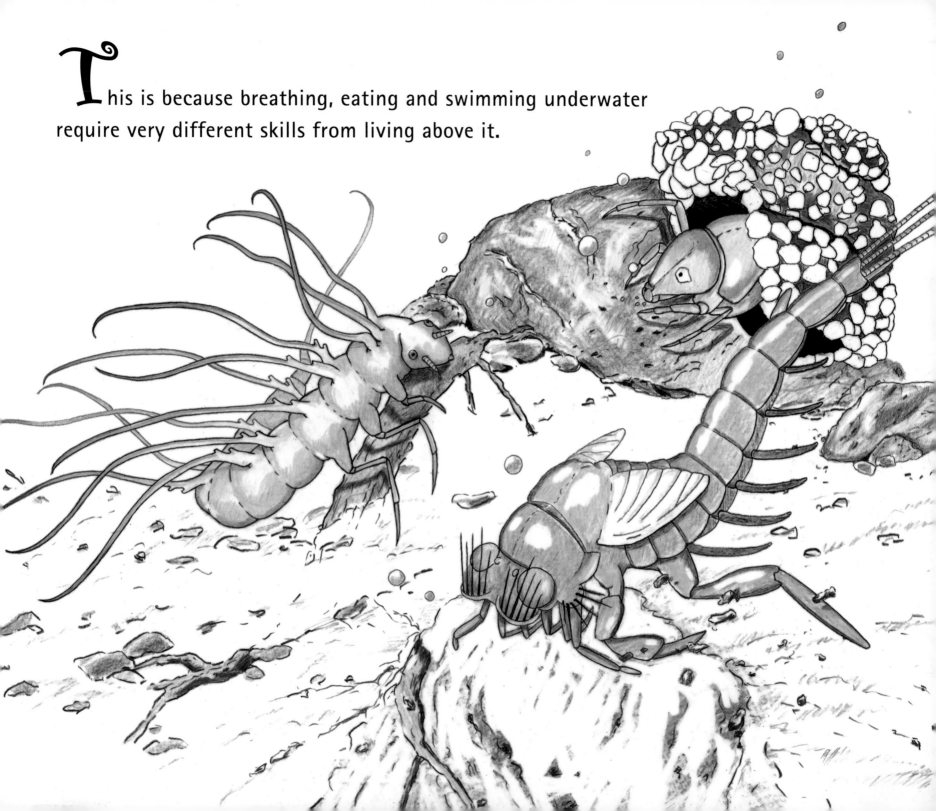

This is because breathing, eating and swimming underwater require very different skills from living above it.

This is a young mayfly. It lives underwater for two or three years. It has three long tails and feathery gills on its abdomen for breathing. This mayfly is sharing its home with the larva of a Tiger salamander.

mayfly naiad

adult mayfly

The adult mayfly lives for only ninety minutes! It is called a mayfly because in May thousands of adults emerge from the water at the same time. The Cutthroat trout living in this river have a good meal that day.

dragonfly naiad

This is a young dragonfly. It lives underwater for three or four years. It has a special mask to feed on other insects in the pond. This naiad is using its mask to catch tiny bitterlings.

The adult dragonfly lives for only three or four weeks. Its six legs form a basket for catching insects in flight. See it swoop down on these mosquitoes!

adult dragonfly

This is a young damselfly. It is smaller and more delicate than a young dragonfly. It also has a mask for catching food. It has three leaf-like tails to help it breathe underwater. See how it lies in wait, hoping to catch its dinner.

damselfly naiad

adult damselfly

The adult damselfly is smaller and more delicate than the adult dragonfly. Instead of catching insects in flight, it prefers to sneak up on them as they rest. These hover flies are in great danger!

stonefly naiad

This is a young stonefly. It lives underwater for one or two years before becoming an adult. It has two tails and fuzzy gills on its thorax for breathing underwater. Here it is swimming with a school of perch.

The adult stonefly got its name because it often sits on stones at the water's edge. These ferns give it a cool place to rest.

adult stonefly

This is a young fishfly. It has long, finger-like gills on its abdomen for breathing underwater. It has big jaws for chewing up other insects, like the scud it has caught today.

fishfly larva

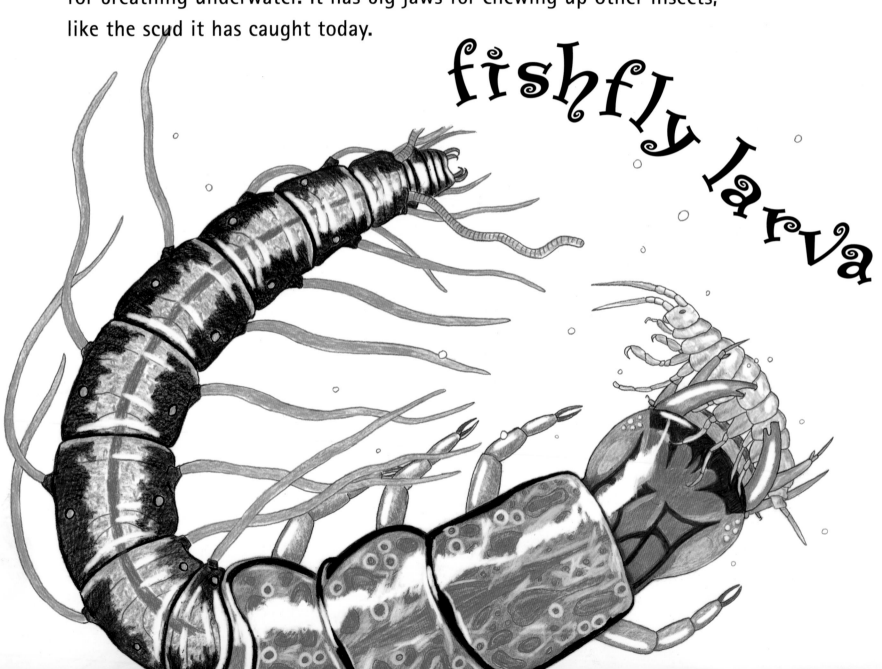

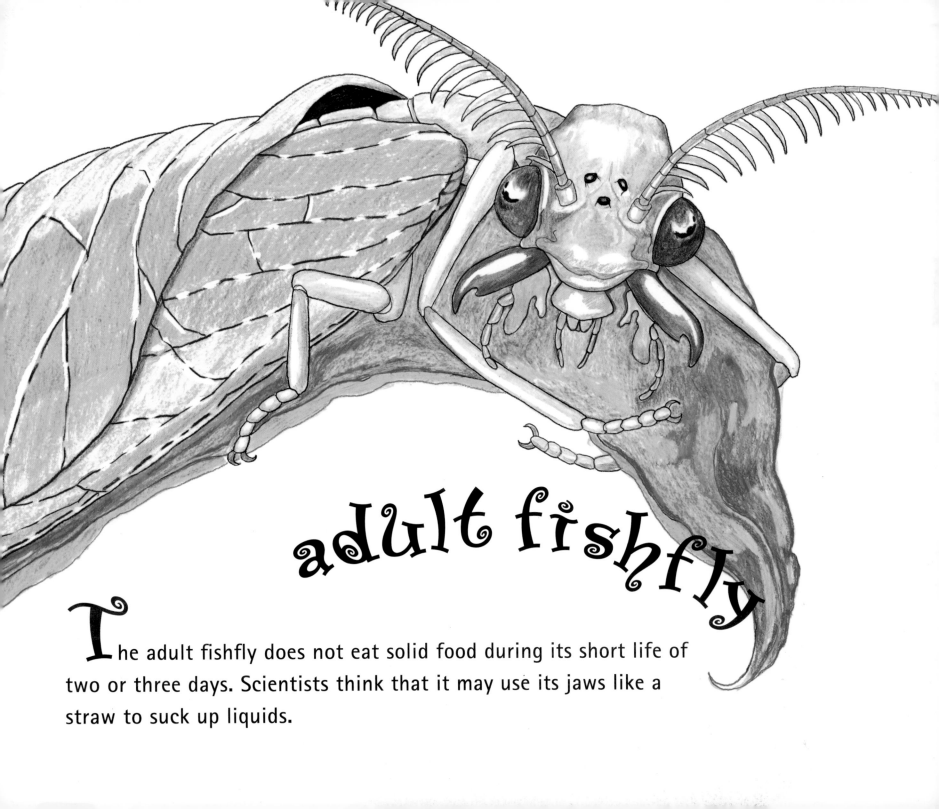

adult fishfly

The adult fishfly does not eat solid food during its short life of two or three days. Scientists think that it may use its jaws like a straw to suck up liquids.

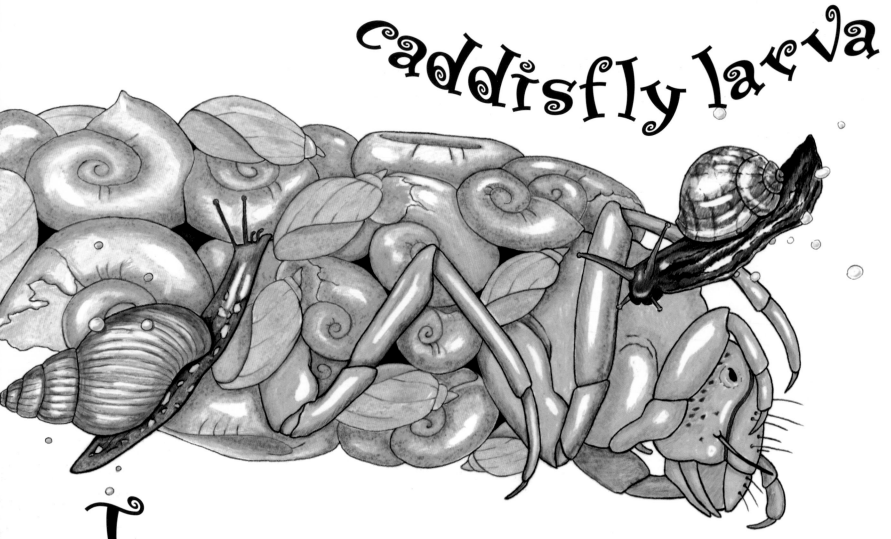

This is a young caddisfly. It spends its underwater life hiding in protective homes called cases. It makes these cases from things it finds such as pebbles, pine needles or empty snail shells. An agate snail and an edible snail are sharing this caddisfly's underwater habitat.

The adult caddisfly looks like a moth. Its wings are covered with thousands of tiny hairs. Look how long its antennae are! It uses them for smelling, tasting and touching.

adult caddisfly

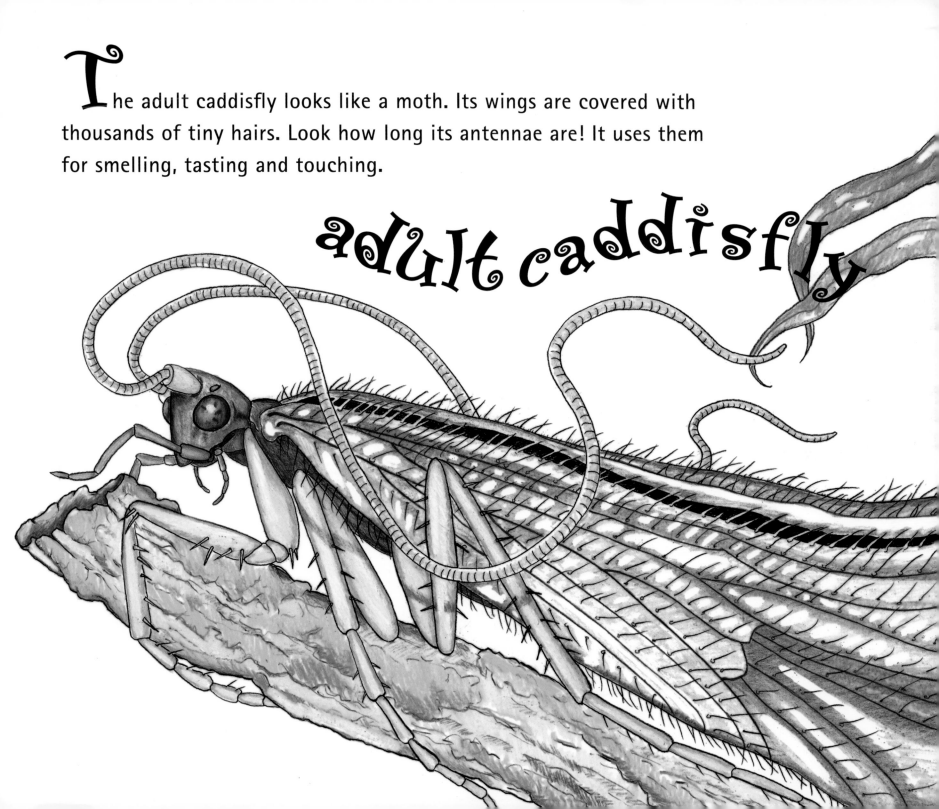

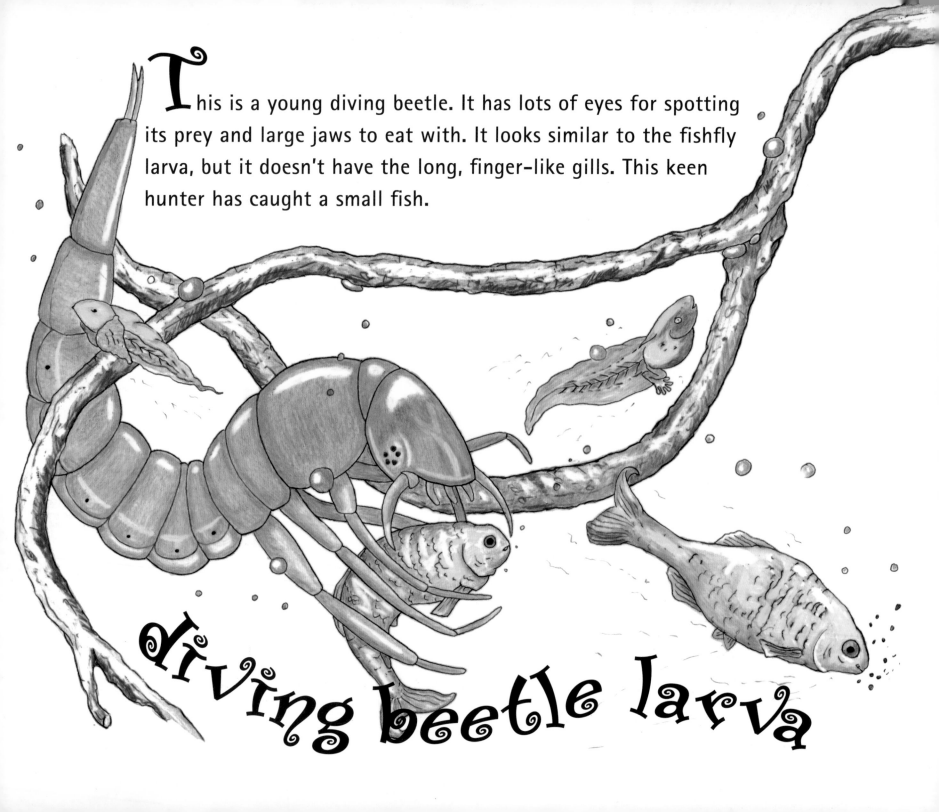

This is a young diving beetle. It has lots of eyes for spotting its prey and large jaws to eat with. It looks similar to the fishfly larva, but it doesn't have the long, finger-like gills. This keen hunter has caught a small fish.

diving beetle larva

adult diving beetle

The adult diving beetle is flat and smooth which helps it swim through the water quickly. It uses its hind legs like paddles. Look at how it races toward this tree frog! It is the only insect in this book that lives underwater as both a larva and an adult.

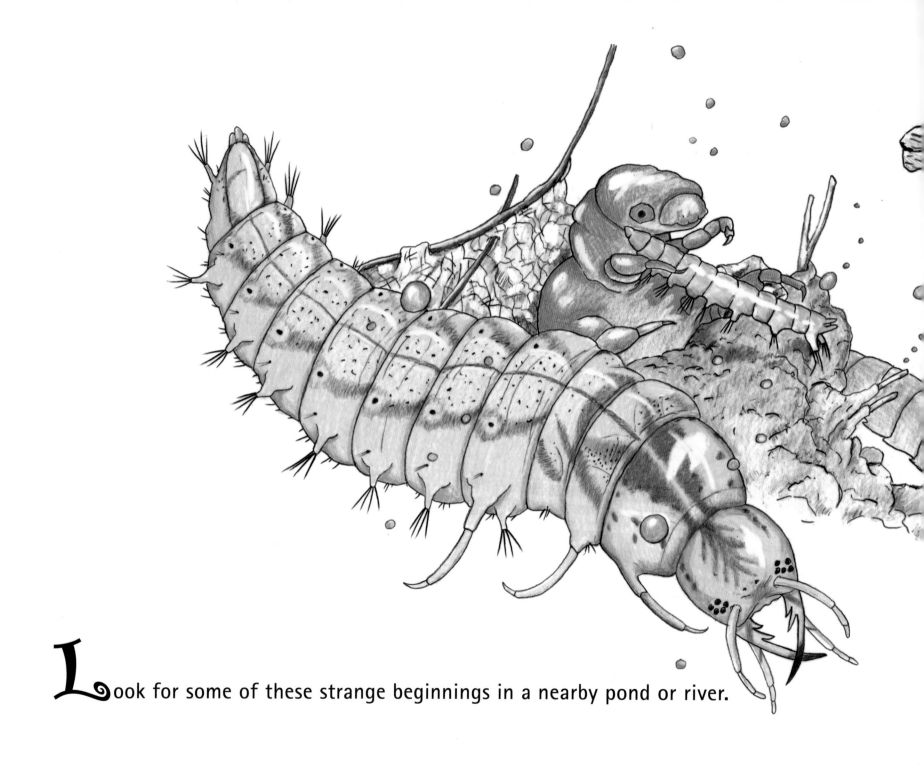

Look for some of these strange beginnings in a nearby pond or river.

Mayflies, dragonflies, damselflies and stoneflies exhibit incomplete metamorphosis. Young insects with this type of life cycle are called naiads. When it is time for them to change from aquatic naiads into terrestrial adults, they swim to the surface or crawl up a plant stem, split down the back, and emerge in their new form.

Mayflies

ORDER EPHEMEROPTERA (EPHEMEROS=EPHEMERAL; PTERON=WING)

Mayfly naiads are found in both standing and running water, usually of very good quality since many species are sensitive to pollutants. Most naiads are herbivores and feed on plant material. The adults live for a very short time and do not feed at all.

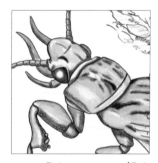 

Ephemeroptera / Ephemeridae / *Hexagenia limbata*

Dragonflies & Damselflies

ORDER ODONATA (ODONTOS=TOOTH)

Dragonfly and damselfly naiads live in permanent standing water. Both naiads and adults are predators. Naiads feed on insects and other arthropods such as water fleas. Adults feed on flying insects like mosquitoes and midges, helping to reduce the population of these pests.

 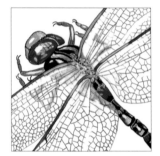    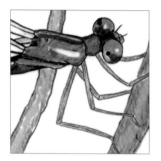

Odonata / Aeshnidae / *Aeshna multicolor* or "Blue-eyed Darner"   Odonata / Lestidae / *Lestes scalaris* or "Dusty Spreadwing"

Stoneflies

ORDER PLECOPTERA (PLEKEIN=FOLD; PTERON=WING)

Stonefly naiads are found in clean, cool, running water. Naiads and adults may be herbivores or predators. The large size of some species makes them ideal models for fly fishers' lures.

Plecoptera / Pteronarcyidae / *Pteronarcys californica* or "Giant Stonefly"

Fishflies, caddisflies and diving beetles undergo a complete metamorphosis. Insects with this type of life cycle are called larvae. Rather than directly changing from a larva to an adult, they have a resting and reorganizing stage known as a pupa. During this stage an amazing transformation takes place, which is still not completely understood by scientists.

Fishflies
ORDER MEGALOPTERA (MEGALOS=LARGE; PTERON=WING)

Fishfly larvae live either in flowing water or small pools of still water. They are voracious predators and feed on other aquatic insects. Their large size and active nature make them popular bait for fly fishing.

Megaloptera / Corydalidae / *Chauliodes pectinicornis*

Caddisflies

ORDER TRICHOPTERA (TRICHOS=HAIR; PTERON=WING)

Caddisfly larvae are usually associated with running freshwater. Each species builds its own unique type of case (caddis=case). Most species are herbivores both as larvae and as adults.

Trichoptera / Helicopsychidae / *Halesochila taylori*

Diving Beetles

ORDER COLEOPTERA (KOLEOS=SHEATH; PTERON=WING)

Diving beetles are found in every type of aquatic habitat. Most species are predators both as larvae and as adults. Adults live underwater and breathe from an air bubble which they carry around with them. They must return to the surface every few hours to renew their oxygen supply.

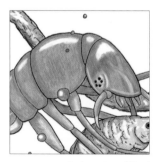 

Coleoptera / Dytiscidae / *Dytiscus dauricus*

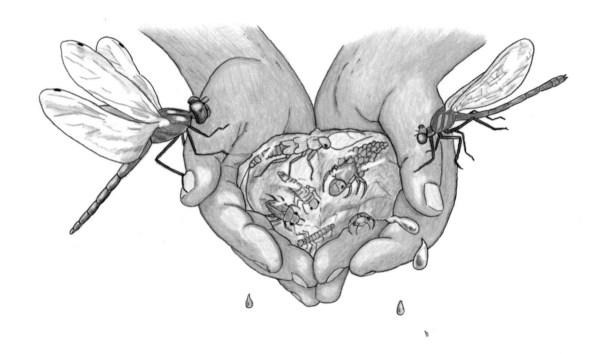

All of the insects in this book could fit in the palm of your hand.